written by
Daphne McMenemy

illustrated by
Toby Price

Gracie's Field Trip

BEAN BOOKS
CURIOSITY · CREATIVITY · DISCOVERY

This book belongs to

_____

For Eli,
who, every single day,
reminds me
of the magic of learning.

It was Monday morning, and it was time for school. Today was

field trip day!

Gracie was so excited. She ran to meet Edie at the bus stop "I've never been to the science centre before!" Gracie said excitedly. "Me neither," Edie replied. "I just wish we could bring Turbo with us," Gracie said.

Turbo was their class pet and one of Gracie's favourite things about school.

"Gracie," Edie giggled. "Don't be silly! Tortoises can't go on field trips!"

Gracie loved field trips! They were exciting adventures where she could explore new places and learn new things. This summer, Gracie visited an amazing place filled with spaceships, rockets, and space vehicles. She learned that the Milky Way galaxy had 100 billion stars.

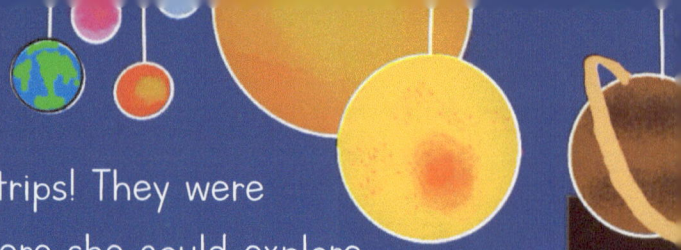

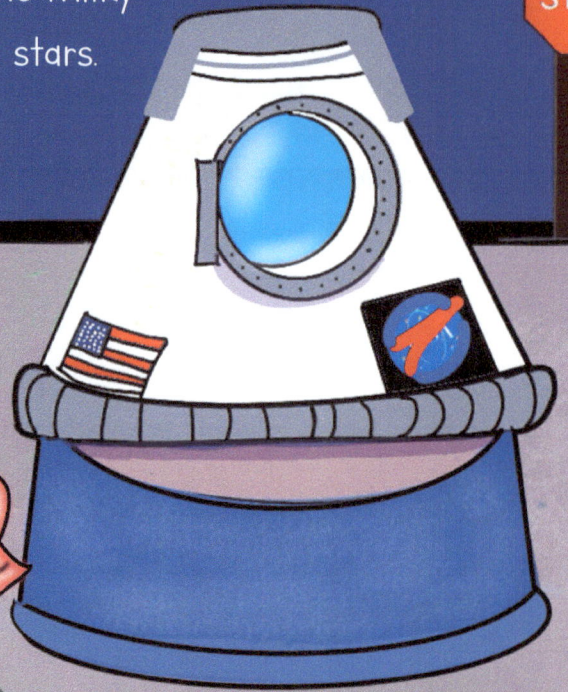

STOP

Two summers ago, she visited an amazing place called an animal sanctuary. She learned that animals there needed a safe place to live. The rescue workers help injured animals get better and make other animal friends.

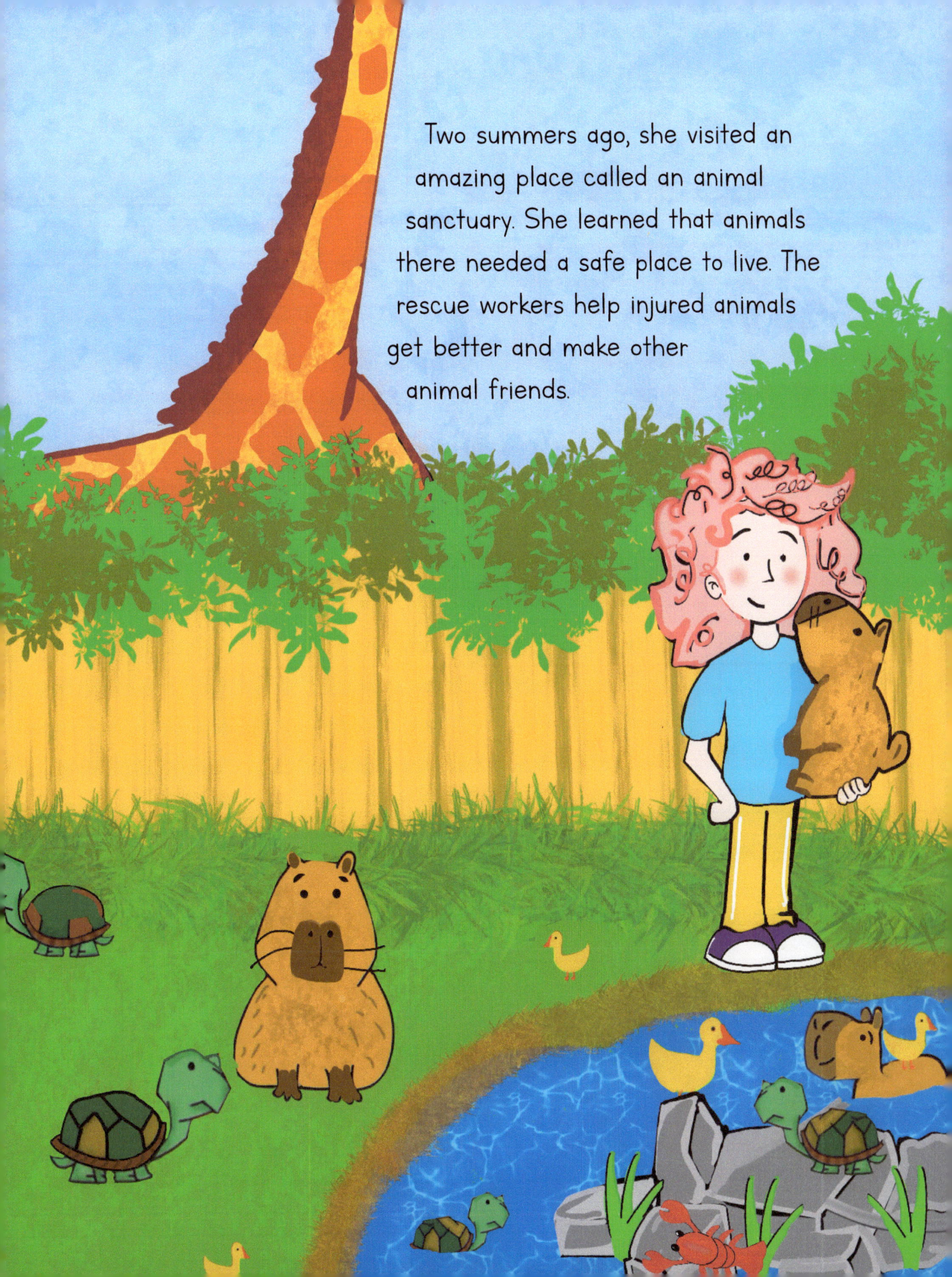

When the bus arrived at the science centre, Gracie and Edie were bursting with excitement. They looked out the window at the huge building. They couldn't wait to get off the bus.

"Follow me, everyone!" Ms. Wilde sang at the class. One by one they hopped off the bus and followed her up the big staircase.

Gracie and Edie looked around in amazement. They unfolded the map Ms. Wilde gave them and immediately started pointing at the symbols they saw. "Gracie! There's an entire exhibit on the solar system!" Edie said as she pointed to the planet.

SCIENCE CENTRE MAP

Ms. Wilde gathered the class and explained that they would spend the day exploring each exhibit, becoming scientists, engineers, mathematicians, and artists. "And there's a surprise waiting for us at the end of the day!" she said.

"We're going to follow the map!" Ms. Wilde led the class down the hall to a great big room called The Robotics Lab in the Physics and Engineering Exhibit.

"And remember, stay together!"

They entered the lab, staring with wonder at the blinking lights and buzzing sounds all around them. There were robots **everywhere**. And in the corner of the room, there was a giant robotic arm.

"Robots are machines that help humans complete tasks," Ms. Wilde said. "Today we're going to program one of these robots to move through a maze."

"Your job is to move your robot through the maze without hitting any obstacles."

Edie, who was always **tinkering**, carefully placed the obstacles around the grid, mapping out a path for the robot to follow. Gracie, who loved **problem-solving**, began programming the robot to follow Edie's path.

Just as their robot was about to complete its maze, the giant robotic arm in the corner of the lab started beeping. The sound startled the girls and they turned towards the noise. The arm began picking up computer parts scattered around it and stacking them in strange piles.

"**Gracie! It's moving!**" Edie exclaimed.

"What's it doing?" Gracie asked.

Gracie and Edie watched closely. Then Edie pushed a button on the control panel.

"Maybe this will fix it," she said.

The arm stopped moving, a green light blinked twice, and it started right back up again. They continued to inspect it determined to figure out how to stop the malfunctioning arm.

"We should ask Ms. Wilde for help," Gracie suggested.

As Gracie turned around, she quickly realized that she and Edie were the only two people left in the lab.

"**Where is everyone?**" Gracie asked.

"I don't know," Edie replied as she looked around.

Gracie and Edie had been so focused on the robotic arm that they hadn't noticed Ms. Wilde leave.

"Gracie, we need to find Ms. Wilde! What should we do?"

"Let's look at the map," Gracie said as she unfolded it and headed out into the hallway.

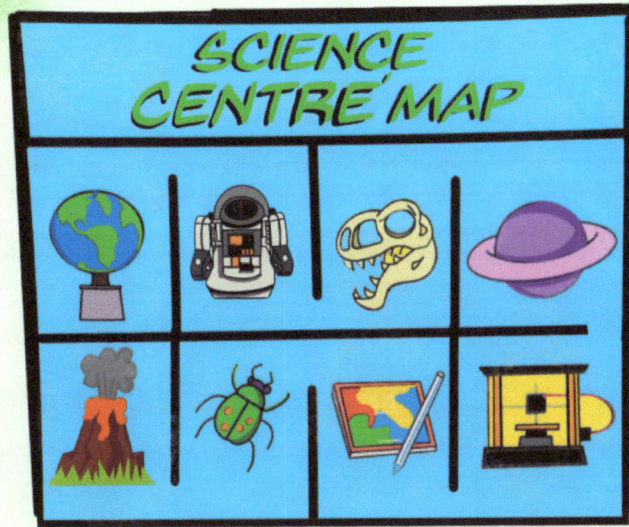

"Ms. Wilde said we'd be following the map. They must be in the Earth Sciences Exhibit!"

Gracie and Edie looked up from the map to find a little girl they didn't recognize.

"Hi! I'm Eli! You look like you might need some help."

"I'm Gracie, and this is Edie. We need to find our teacher."

"Do you know where the Earth Sciences Exhibit is?" Edie asked.

"I do. I know where every exhibit is," Eli answered.

"You do? How?" Edie asked.

"This place belongs to my grandmother. She loves learning and exploring. When she was a little girl, she used to take clocks apart so she could find out how they worked! She always wanted to have an entire building filled with stuff so she could spend all day learning how things worked. I've been coming here my whole life."

And with that, Eli turned around and announced, "The exhibit is this way!"

The girls followed Eli down a long hallway. Turning the corner, Eli said, "Welcome to Earth Sciences!"

Gracie looked around. "But Ms. Wilde isn't here," she frowned.

"Maybe she was here. Let's look for clues," Edie said hopefully.

Gracie and Edie looked around at the fossils and dinosaur skeletons.

"What's that?" Gracie asked.

"That's a microraptor," Eli answered. "They were dinosaurs with feathers! And that's its fossil."

Edie dusted off a rock with a footprint in it.

"Footprint fossils are like stamps pressed into the ground a really long time ago," Eli explained. "Scientists study the paths dinosaurs walked by looking at the directions of the footprints."

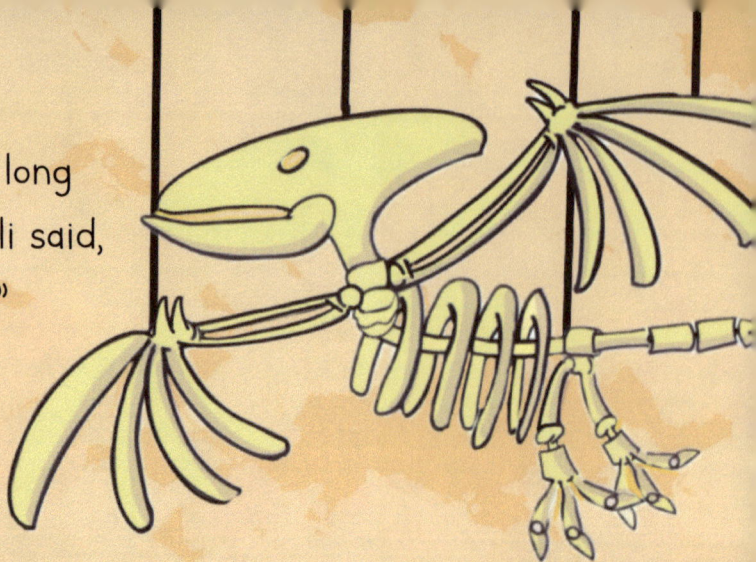

"Look!" Gracie pointed to the dusty footprints on the floor. "I think Ms. Wilde **WAS** here!"

Edie looked at the map. The footprints were heading towards the Space and Astronomy Exhibit.

They looked at Eli, who said, " **Follow the footprints!** "

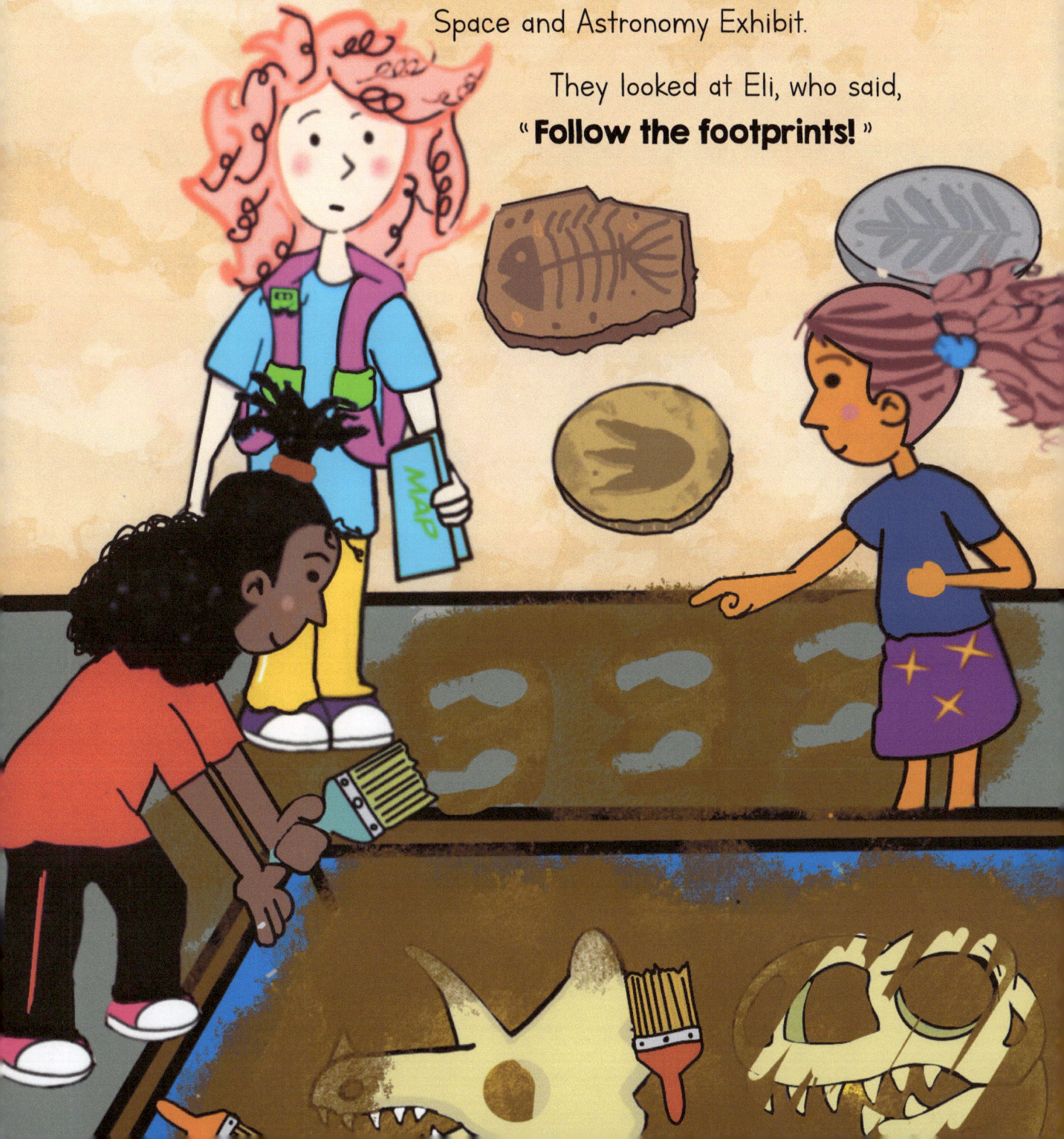

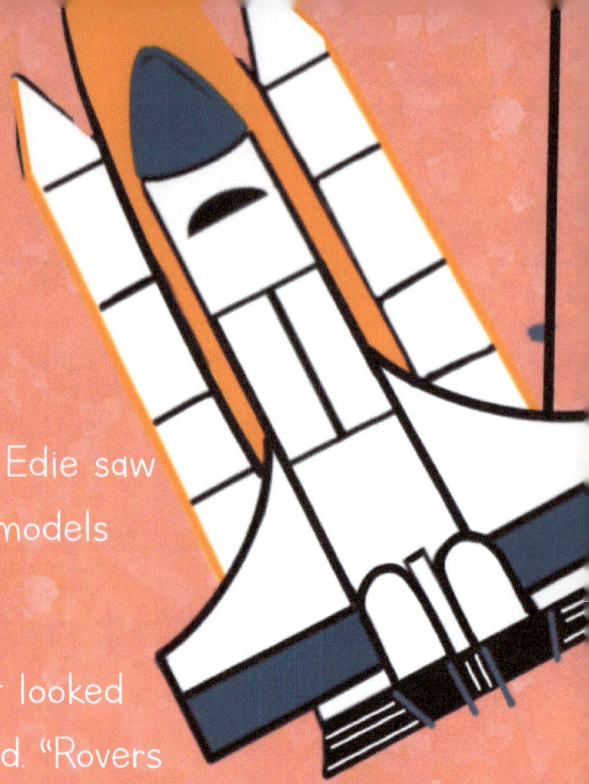

The map led the girls to the planetarium. Edie saw satellites and star charts. Gracie noticed models of rockets and space shuttles.

"What's that?" Gracie pointed to cars that looked like robots. "Those are rovers," Eli explained. "Rovers are robotic vehicles sent to space to explore planets and asteroids."

Edie noticed an obstacle course on the floor. There were mini rovers following paths made with arrows to get around rocks.

"That rover is called Perseverance. It explores craters on Mars. It collects samples to bring back to Earth for scientists to study."

"Look!" Gracie pointed to the arrows on the course. "I think whoever was here created a path to the next exhibit!"

Edie pulled out the map. The arrows were pointing towards the Technology and Innovation Exhibit.

" **Follow the arrows!** "

Gracie and Edie followed Eli, hoping to find their teacher. What they found instead were computers and machines everywhere! The machines were buzzing and humming.

"It's GoBot!" Gracie pointed to a picture of their classroom robot on a computer screen.

"What's GoBot doing here?" Edie asked.

"That's a 3D design for the printer." Eli pointed to the machines next to the computer. "They create real objects using all kinds of materials like plastic, metal, clay, and even food!"

Edie picked up a roll of something that looked like bright green string. "That's filament," Eli said. "It's what this 3D printer uses to build objects. The printer melts the filament and then pushes it out to build the object."

Gracie realized all of the machines were printing 3D models of GoBot. That's when she saw a trail of bright green filament leading to the Art-Science Exhibit.

Eli was already on her way. **"Follow the filament!"**

Eli led the girls to a room filled with colourful paintings of caribou, bears, and turtles.

"Is that a painting, too?" Gracie pointed to a piece of artwork that looked like it was made on a computer. "Sure is!" Eli answered. "Some artists paint on computers. They experiment with different colours and different brushes."

"Artists paint to share their feelings and tell stories," Eli explained.

Edie was looking at a freshly painted picture of Turbo. "I think Ms. Wilde was here!"

That's when Gracie noticed drops of paint on the floor.

Edie looked at the map. The paint drops were leading to the Biology and Life Sciences Exhibit.

"**Follow the paint!**"

Gracie and Edie followed Eli down another hallway, certain they'd see Ms. Wilde. What they saw instead were walls lined with insect displays. "Welcome to Insect World!" Eli exclaimed.

"There's an entire exhibit dedicated to insects?" Gracie asked.

"There is!" Eli explained, "Insects are a really important part of our environment. Each one has an important job!"

"What strange-looking birdhouses!" Edie said as she picked up a little wooden house.

"That's a bug hotel!" Eli's face lit up. "We need bugs to help our plants grow. They protect the plants and keep the soil healthy! Bug hotels give those insects a safe place to live."

Gracie noticed a trail of pinecones and branches. "These bug hotels must belong to our class! They were here!"

The trail led right out the door. Edie took out her map. "We need to get to the Chemistry Lab."

All three girls looked at one another.

"Follow the trail!"

Gracie and Edie marvelled at the test tubes and beakers filled with colourful liquids, swirling around the containers.

"Is that lava?" Gracie pointed to a volcano. There was liquid bubbling over the top of it.

"That's a model volcano," Eli explained. "When different liquids and solids mix together, it creates a chemical reaction. Baking soda and vinegar make bubbles. The bubbling comes from carbon dioxide gas, and the bubbles flow like lava!"

"It's like a mini eruption!" Edie said.

"The lava is spilling across the floor!" Gracie said excitedly!
With her map in her hand, Edie said, "It leads to the Robotics Lab."

"The Robotics Lab?" Gracie asked. "We were already there. Do you think Ms. Wilde is back there?"

The girls looked at Eli.
"There's only one way to find out!"

As they walked down the hallway, they heard a voice they recognized. The girls looked at one another, smiling ear to ear. "That's Ms. Wilde!"

"I guess my job here is done!" Eli said as they approached the Robotics Lab.

"Eli, thank you so much for helping us!" Gracie said.
"Thanks to you, we learned so much on this field trip!" Edie added.

"You're welcome!" she replied to her new friends. "I'd better go and find my grandmother!" And just like that, Eli was off.

The girls walked into the lab where they found Ms. Wilde standing beside the robotic arm assembling a small robotic turtle. "**Surprise!**" she called out as she held it up for the girls to see.

"**A robot Turbo!**" Gracie said. The robotic arm hadn't been malfunctioning after all. It had been programmed to build their surprise.

"I guess tortoises **do** go on field trips!" Edie giggled.

Ms. Wilde led the class out of the science centre.

She smiled at Gracie and Edie and said, "I hope you girls had fun today! We learned so much, didn't we?"

"We sure did!" they said.

And then with a wink Ms. Wilde replied, **"And thank goodness for that map!"**

BFF

Science
Centre
Memories

#Robots

Gracie and Eli

Best Class Pet Ever!

Robot Turbo!

Me and Eli

Tortoises DO go on field trips!

Best Field Trip Ever!

Women in STEM

Dr. Swati Mohan is a scientist and engineer who helped NASA land a robot on Mars. She worked on the Perseverance rover, which explores the red planet. She's an inspiring leader who shows how teamwork makes big dreams possible.

Autumn Smith, also known as **Mishiikenh Kwe**, is an Anishinaabe artist, water protector, and activist. She works to keep water clean and safe for everyone. Her efforts remind us to respect nature and protect our environment. Autumn's artwork is featured in the Art-Science Exhibit that Gracie, Edie, and Eli visit.

Dr. Jessica Ware is an entomologist who studies dragonflies and other insects. She loves learning how insects live and how they've changed over millions of years. Her work helps us understand the important role bugs play in nature.

Jennifer A. Lewis is an inventor and scientist who creates amazing 3D-printed materials. Her work helps make new tools for medicine, like printing tiny devices to help heal the body. She shows how science and creativity go hand in hand.

Dr. Tessa Lau is a computer scientist who loves building robots that help people with everyday tasks. She created a company to make robots smarter and easier to use. Her work helps make technology more helpful in our daily lives.

Dr. Betty Wright Harris is a chemist who made important discoveries to keep people safe from dangerous chemicals. She also works to inspire young scientists. Her passion for science helps protect the world.

Dr. Jingmai O'Connor is a paleontologist who studies ancient birds and dinosaurs. She travels the world to look for fossils and learn about life millions of years ago. Her discoveries teach us how birds evolved from dinosaurs.

Daphne McMenemy is an award-winning Canadian educator, author, and speaker with a passion for inspiring curiosity, creativity, and a love of learning. She is best known for her Gracie series, which introduces young readers to coding, problem-solving, and the power of perseverance. Through her books and work in education, Daphne empowers students and teachers to embrace innovation and make meaningful connections through technology.

Learn more about Daphne at www.daphnemcmenemy.com.

Learn more about Gracie at www.discovergracie.com.

First published in Canada in 2024.
This edition published by Bean Books in 2025.

Copyright © 2025 Daphne McMenemy
Illustrations © 2024 Toby Price

**The Future Belongs
to the Innovators**